MANSA'S Little REMINDERS

The Money Workbook for Kids

PART 1

Written by A.D. Williams &
Kendal Fordham

Illustrated by Taylor Bou

For information regarding permissions, contact the publisher at:
www.MansasLittleReminders.com

Author: A.D. Williams and Kendal Fordham Illustrator: Taylor Bou

ISBN: 9781736168929

Published in the United States of America
Printed in the United States of America

Table of Contents

Welcome, Parents, Educators and Leaders

Thank you for investing in your children. If you're like us, you know how important financial literacy and money management are. We live in a world that revolves around money. Right or wrong, we need to be aware that managing our money or creating wealth can provide more opportunities for ourselves and our children.

Our goal with this workbook is to continue introducing children to the basics of money management in a fun and interactive way. Along with our first book *Mansa's Little Reminders*, we are committed to unlocking the wealth creator in kids everywhere and level the financial odds for generations to come.

Early Learning + Fun = A Lifetime of Wealth

Handling money is a learned behavior. About 80% of millionaires are the first generation in their families to have wealth.

1

FROM HERE ON OUT, THIS IS FOR THE KIDS,
BUT THEY WILL NEED YOUR HELP!

Printables and other resources are available at:

www.MansasLittleReminders.com search resources. While many of the

activities are created to help children learn on their own, adult supervision

and positive reinforcement are necessary to enhance your child's

learning experience.

Welcome, Kids

Welcome, friends! Our team here at *Mansa's Little Reminders* created this workbook for YOU and YOUR future. Do you know what financial freedom or financial independence means? Well, it means different things to different people, but here are a few benefits of having financial independence:

- Not having to ask your parents, or anyone, for money

- Having enough income to pay your living expenses for the rest of your life without depending on others

- Having enough money to help a friend or charity

In general, it means being prepared. And when you're prepared for anything, you will be self-reliant. If you take this information seriously, you will be one step closer to financial freedom, success, and wealth—way faster than most people in the world.

In this workbook, you will experience examples to learn how to do the following:

- Use your money in smart ways through budgeting so that you never run out

- Save money and not waste it so that you always have some available to you when you need it or want it

- Make money on your own by working smart and being your own boss through entrepreneurship

DON'T BE AFRAID to ask your parents, teachers, or friends for help. Also, Mansa, Mark, Cuzzo, Mom, and Uncle Craig from our first book *Mansa's Little Reminders* will help you along the way. Get excited to make money, save money, and move one step closer to financial freedom!

SECTION 1

Budgeting:

We Don't Have Both Money

*"We don't have both money, and you need to
understand what that means."*

—Mom

BUDGETING - A budget is an estimate of income and expenses for a set period of time. It's a plan for how much you will save and spend over that period, usually a month or year. The key is don't spend more than you make.

Vocabulary Words:

BUDGET – An organized and detailed list of income and expenses for a given period of time. This is the best way to organize your money and make it work for you.

INCOME – Revenue (money) received for goods or services, or from other sources like a job or selling something. We use income to fund day-to-day spending.

MONEY – A medium of exchange that people and global economies willingly accept as payment for current or future transactions.

VALUE – What something is worth to you.

MANSA'S TIP:

Think of your favorite movie or cartoon. Imagine you are an actor. Act out scenes by using each vocabulary word in your skits. Have fun!

Exercise 1
A Kid's Gotta Eat!

What's your favorite meal in the whole wide world? Not something from a restaurant, but something that is homemade from someone you care about. Like a meal your grandmother would make.

1. Go to www.MansasLittleReminders.com and print off the money sheet under resources.

2. Cut out, color, and label enough bills to purchase the ingredients for the home-cooked meal.

3. Have an adult gather or buy the ingredients for the meal and label each one with a price.

4. Create your own mini store in the comfort of your kitchen or family room! Remember, it doesn't need to be fancy.

5. With your money and recipe in hand, buy what you need to make your favorite meal!

6. Once you purchase the items, organize the other kitchen items you will need to use and begin preparing and cooking the meal. Enjoy!

DON'T WORRY if this exercise is confusing or even scary. Take your time, have fun and do the best you can. If you're not the best chef, just give it a try and you might be surprised. Remember, failure is part of the process of becoming successful!

We would love to see your finished meal. Tale a picture or video and briefly explain what this project meant to you. Post it on your social media accounts and tag us for a feature! @mansaslittlereminders

Exercise 2
Now Let's Budget!

The below chart represents a budget. Each slice represents a precentage of income to be spent on that category. Check it out.

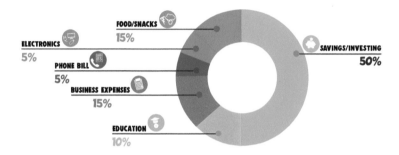

Each category represents something that you need or want. For example, you may love video games, snacks, or movies, but you also want to start saving for something special. A budget is an important tool that will help you understand where your money is going and will allow you to keep more money.

What are examples of daily spending in your household? It is your turn to make a budget just for you. Imagine you have $100. Write in categories and a dollar amount for each. Remember you cannot use more than $100.

MANSA'S TIP:

Ask a parent to help you to understand the household budget. Visit the resources section at www.MansasLittleReminders.com to print out a blank budget pie chart.

SECTION 2

Saving:

Acorns

"If you like money, you should think about how to find it, how to take care of it, and not waste it like you do with my acorns. Life is a lot sweeter if you can find your acorns!"

—*Mansa*

18

Vocabulary Words:

GOALS – Measurable milestones that you work toward every day. It is always a good idea to write down your goals, whether it be for the day, week, month, year, or even longer.

SAVINGS – The act of setting money aside for the future. It is always good to have six months of monthly bills saved as cash in your savings account. This way, when emergencies come up, you're prepared!

PRICE – An amount that is expected or required to be paid for a good or service.

SALE – When a seller or owner of a good or service offers those goods or services at a reduced price.

Write down your savings goals and other goals with intention. I write mine on my bathroom mirror with a dry erase marker and read them every day when I wake up and when I go to bed.

Exercise 1
Goal Setting Through a Vision Board

For many people, goals start with a vision. It is believed that the more thought put toward a vision, the higher the chance of achieving it in life. Where do you see yourself in 5 years? 10 years? 30 years? It is time to dream! Where do you want to live and what does it look like? What type of car do you drive? Do you have children? Are you married? What do you do for work? Do you live in the mountains or by the ocean? Do you have a big house with a lot of rooms or a small home with a lot of land? How much money do you have in your savings account?

Ask an adult for magazines they don't need anymore. Use magazines that have pictures of the things in your vision.

1. Cut out the pictures of all the things you would like in your life. The cars, house, vacations. Anything you desire should be added to your vision board. (If you can't find the pictures in magazines, print out pictures from websites that you and your parents find.)

2. Glue the pictures onto a piece of cardboard in any order, shape, or size.

3. Write your name across the top.

4. Add to the vision board at any time.

Let's envision Mansa, the talking squirrel from *Mansa's Little Reminders* book, just gave you some money. You invested the money, and over time that money grew and was enough for you to buy one thing on your vision board. A bike, car, vacation, or anything else on your vision board.

Sounds like a dream, right?

Well, it isn't. This is what you can achieve by saving and investing your money, not spending it!

 MANSA'S TIP:

If you invested 10% of everything you earned, you would see how your savings would grow without missing that money.

Hang your vision board in your room or a place you can look at it every day. Share your vision and savings goals with your family. Talk about it often. See it, believe it, and you will live it!

Exercise 2

Failure Fridays

We live in a world that is so focused on success, it's easy to forget that success is usually built on experiencing failures. The word "failure" has such a negative feeling associated with it. We need to adjust the way we think about failure!

Failure without learning is like walking on a treadmill. You're moving but not going anywhere. But learning from failure leads to success. Most successful people have failed several times in their lives.

Which is worse, trying something and failing but then learning from the failure, or not trying something at all?

Each time you fail, ask yourself these three questions. Then write down the answers on a piece of paper.

- What will I do differently next time?
- What will I do the same?
- What did I learn from this experience?

Finally, explain to someone in your group of friends or family how you failed, how you'll try again but what you'll do differently, what you'll do the same, and what you learned.

MANSA'S TIP:

Each Friday, take a moment to reflect on what happened that week. Look at your successes and failures from each week and challenge yourself to honor your successes and not repeat any mistakes. Remember:

- **It's okay to fail as long as you are learning lessons.**

- **Everyone fails.**

- **You are successful for just trying new things!**

SECTION 3

Entrepreneurship:

The Lemonade Stand

*I really love lemonade, and I think I want to learn how to make some so I can
sell it to people. That way I can buy my own games and stuff. I don't know,
maybe if I make enough, I can help you out, too."*

—*Mark*

ENTREPRENEUR BUSINESS PLAN
30-SECOND SUMMARY

Vocabulary Words:

ENTREPRENEUR – Someone who creates and operates a business. Also known as self-employed, a person who makes a living by working for themself.

BUSINESS PLAN – Document that describes a company's structure, who they serve, what they provide, where they provide it, how they tell people about what they do, and how much money they plan to make.

30-SECOND SUMMARY – A short and to-the-point speech that tells someone else about what you do. This speech should not last longer than a typical ride in an elevator, about 30 seconds.

There are many different paths to consider when thinking about a career. You can work for someone or work for yourself. There are pros and cons for each, and it's difficult to plan ahead on which path you will follow. For now, just focus on doing your best in school and earn a degree to give yourself the most options and opportunities to choose from. When the time is right, you will be in a better situation to decide which career path is best for you.

In this section, we will be discussing what's involved in becoming an entrepreneur. When you start and manage your own business, you are responsible for everything. The rewards for being an entrepreneur can be tremendous, and you will learn the meaning of hard work.

Understanding basic business language, money management, and **smart work*** at an early age gives you an important head start.

 **MANSA'S TIP:**

*Working smart means using your time wisely. Many people think the only way to get more money is to get more jobs working for other people! This may be the easiest way, but it might not be the best way. With a similar amount of effort, you may be able to make more money working for yourself, especially if you have your own business in addition to your main job.

Exercise 1
Business Planning

A business plan is like using a roadmap or GPS to find your way to a location you have never been to before. It's similar to using an outline for writing a paper. It organizes your thoughts and puts down all the necessary components for starting, running and being successful in your business. It gives you direction and focus and should be as detailed as possible.

Hopefully, a business plan keeps you from making unnecessary mistakes along the way and is one of the first tools that goes into the tool belt of a successful entrepreneur.

BUSINESS PLAN
ROAD DIRECTIONS

MANSA'S TIP:

Your business plan is your road map.

The Lemonade Stand
Mark's One-Page Business Plan

Here is an example of a business plan using a young boy by the name of Mark. He started a lemonade stand with the help of his mom and his cousin Cuzzo. Read through Mark's plan before you complete yours.

OVERVIEW

What will you sell?

- Fresh lemonade

Who will buy it?

- Anyone who loves lemonade and fruit snacks
- Customers in town and from everywhere, thanks to the internet

How will your business idea help others?

- Hydration
- Health
- Easy-to-find location
- Customers feel good supporting small businesses

MONEY

How much will you charge?

- $2 for lemonade and $1 for snacks

How will you get paid?

- Cash
- Venmo

How else can you make money from this project?

- Sell healthy fruit snacks or homemade cookies or cakes to go with the lemonade

MARKETING

How will customers learn about your business?

- Being in the same location week after week creates repeat customers.
- Word of mouth
- Post on local bulletin boards
- Post on socail media

How can you encourage referrals?

(People telling other people about your business)

- Provide an outstanding service to everyone
- Offer discounts for referrals
- Offer specials like "Buy 2 get 1 free"
- Make your product stand out by using quality or organic ingredients
- Make location stand out with nice signs and graphics

WINNING

How will you measure success?

(The project will make you happy when it achieves these metrics)

- How much money you make each week, each month, over a year
- The number of customers you sell to
- How many customers are new versus returning
- How many customers are from referrals

OBSTACLES/CHALLENGES

- Sometimes lemonade can be unhealthy with too much sugar.
- Can I sell lemonade at the park or pool without a license?
- Will customers purchase lemonade in a cup?
- Do I need helpers during busy times?

List specific solutions to handle the obstacles mentioned above

- Use honey or agave for lemonade to make it healthier.
- Call city officials or search the internet and check before you set up.
- Be sure to ask your customers what they prefer when you see them and keep their contact information for future questions.
- Practice run: Go sell for a day and monitor sales. Getting extra help may result in more revenue (money).

Remember, this is just an example designed to get you thinking about your business and what is involved in making it successful.

Location is very important! Making sure that your business is seen and located in places where your customers are is important for any business.

Think about the **prices** for what you are selling. Mark searched on Google to see what other people charged for lemonade.

Not everyone carries cash, so offering other **options** will help you increase your sales. Make it **easy** for customers to purchase your products. Make sure you have enough change with you.

Every business will have **obstacles/challenges**. It is important to think about them beforehand and list how you will solve them like Mark did for his lemonade stand.

Your One-Page Business Plan

Now it's your turn to give it a try. Grab a separate sheet of paper and write out your business plan or use the business plan template at www.MansasLittleReminders.com in the resources section. Take as much time as you need.

Here are some cool things to think about before you start writing out your business plan:

Aim for at least three ideas: It's a good idea to have more ideas. Notice that Mark had lemonade and fruit snacks, but he might make a podcast and is even thinking about a mobile lemonade cart.

Be different and creative: Lemonade and fruit snacks are normal. Maybe you have other ideas or inventions.

Location: Think about whether your business idea will be offered online, at the local park, even downtown in the city, or maybe even all the above. The goal is that more people see your business because then more people can buy from you.

Donations: As an entrepreneur, always think about how you can help others and your community. You can do this by donating some of your sales money to charities or people in need.

Payment: Notice that Mark allowed customers to use cash and digital payment like the cash apps, Venmo, Zelle, PayPal, and more. Make it easy for customers to buy your products and services.

Go to **www.MansasLittleReminders.com** and search in the resources section to grab the business template and get started.

Imagine you have $100 to start.

OVERVIEW

- What will you sell?
- Who will buy it?
- How will your business idea help others?

MONEY

- How much will you charge?
- How will you get paid?
- How else will you make money from this project?

MARKETING

- How much will customers learn about your business?
- How can you encourage referrals (people telling their friends about it)?

WINNING

- The project will make you happy when it achieves these metrics:

  Number of customers or annual income

OBSTACLES/CHALLENGES

- What are some obstacles or challenges that could prevent you from winning?

- What are some ways to solve each obstacle or challenge?

Financials

In business and entrepreneurship, the goal is to provide value to your customers and make profit.

Profit = Revenue − Expenses

Revenue = Money made from sales

Expenses = Money spent to run the business

Create a Commerical

@cuzzoshealthyhairproducts

1:36 / 2:06

Cuzzo's Commerical

 30K 0K

Design a 30-second video that describes a business or product that you created.

Dress up in your fanciest business clothes and use props, persuasive language, a confident posture, and hand gestures to create a commercial using either your cell phone or an adult's phone.

Make sure the 30-second video includes the following information.

☐ Your name

☐ Your product

☐ How your product helps people

☐ Good things about your product

☐ What you need from the people you are talking to

MANSA'S TIPS:

Pretend you are your favorite actor. Change the tone of your voice to add drama. Use your hands and body to add feeling and emotion to your speech.

For a more powerful 30-second summary, clearly state a problem in your industry and how your product fixes that problem.

Need commercial ideas? Visit YouTube and search for the best commercials.

Need business ideas? Visit Google, Etsy, Pinterest, or Shopify.

Need podcast ideas? Visit YouTube or check out Patreon.com.

**Always be sure to ask an adult to help
search the internet.**

CONGRATULATIONS ON TAKING A BIG STEP TOWARD YOUR FINANCIAL FREEDOM!

BUDGETING
SAVING
ENTREPRENEURSHIP

....is just the start of our journey.

Connect with us and be the first to know about additional books, workbooks and resources all designed to help you become financially independent.

Visit our website and sign up for our newsletter to receive discounts on purchases.

YOU CAN CONNECT WITH US

@mansaslittlereminders
www.MansasLittleReminders.com

CPSIA information can be obtained
at www.ICGtesting.com
Printed in the USA
LVHW070032300322
714786LV00001B/7